Mommy, Please Don't Cry

THERE ARE NO TEARS IN HEAVEN

By

LINDA DEYMAZ

Artwork by

LAURIE SNOW HEIN

Mommy, Please Don't Cry...
© 2003 by Linda DeYmaz
published by Multnomah Gifts™, a division of Multnomah® Publishers, Inc.
P.O. Box 1720, Sisters, Oregon 97759

ISBN 1-59052-151-X

Artwork © 2003 by Laurie Snow Hein
Artwork designed by Laurie Snow Hein may not be reproduced without permission.
For information regarding art prints featured in this book, contact: artistlsh@aol.com.

Designed by Garborg Design Works, Minneapolis, Minnesota

Scripture quotations are taken from:
The Holy Bible, New International Version
1973, 1984 by International Bible Society,
used by permission of Zondervan Publishing House;
The Living Bible (TLB)
1971. Used by permission of Tyndale House Publishers, Inc.
All rights reserved.;
The Holy Bible, New King James Version (NKJV)
1984 by Thomas Nelson, Inc.

Multnomah is a trademark of Multnomah Publishers, Inc., and is registered in the U.S. Patent and Trademark Office.
The colophon is a trademark of Multnomah Publishers, Inc.

For Information:
MULTNOMAH PUBLISHERS, INC. • P.O. BOX 1720 • SISTERS, OR 97759

Printed in Korea

Library of Congress Cataloging-in-Publication Data

DeYmaz, Linda.
  Mommy, please don't cry : there are no tears in heaven / by Linda
DeYmaz.
     p. cm.
  ISBN 1-59052-151-X
  1. Children--Death--Religious aspects--Christianity. 2.
Bereavement--Religious aspects--Christianity. 3. Mothers--Religious
life. 4. Consolation. I. Title.
  BV4907.D49 2003
  242' .4--dc21

                                                    2003003686

04 05 06 07 08 09—16 15 14 13 12 11 10

IN MEMORY OF MY
PRECIOUS LITTLE GIRL
ALEXANDRA GRACE DEYMAZ,
WHO WENT TO BE
WITH JESUS ON
EASTER MORNING, 1995.
UNTIL I SEE YOU FACE TO FACE,
MOMMY

THIS BOOK IS DEDICATED
TO MOTHERS
EVERYWHERE WHO HAVE
EXPERIENCED
THE DEEP SORROW
OF LOSING A CHILD.

From One Mother to Another

From the moment of conception, we are mothers. From the instant pregnancy is confirmed, we make plans and our dreams unfold. There is the nursery to design and wallpaper to hang; the rocker, the cradle, and the high chair to buy. We spend countless hours looking for just the right name or searching the malls for the perfect baby book. We choose the first outfit, the first toy and teddy bear. And, of course, we watch in delight and amazement as our babies and our waistlines increase!

Then, in a moment's time, our world shatters like fine china. And the darkness comes.

For some it was a phone call from the doctor. Still others were all alone. Perhaps you found your precious baby lifeless in the crib, a heartbeat suddenly stopped. Or maybe, like me, it was in a cold, dark room that you felt life slip away as you watched a black, silent ultrasound.

Our stories are all different, but our pain is the same. We are mothers who will forever grieve the loss of our children. And yet, there is hope for our troubled souls.

It's my prayer that this simple book will satisfy your innermost longing to know that your child is wonderfully alive in heaven. Each thought and illustration has been carefully prepared to help you feel that joy. My desire is that these words and pictures will bring a smile to your face, tears to your eyes, and great healing to your broken heart.

I will always carry a deep sorrow for the loss of my little girl. Yet, in spite of this tragedy, I believe with all my heart that God sent Ali Grace to enrich my life, and to give both you and me a small glimpse of eternity.

With love,

Linda

MOMMY, PLEASE

DON'T CRY...

A BEAUTIFUL ANGEL

CARRIED ME HERE!

I MET JESUS

TODAY, MOMMY!

HE CRADLED ME IN HIS

BIG, STRONG ARMS.

HE MADE ME FEEL SO

HAPPY INSIDE.

"Let the little children come to me, and do not hinder them, for the kingdom of God belongs to such as these."

MOMMY, PLEASE DON'T CRY...

HEAVEN IS WONDERFUL!

DID YOU KNOW THE STREETS

ARE MADE OF GOLD?

REAL GOLD!

I HAVE LOTS

OF FRIENDS, MOMMY.

WE RUN AND PLAY,

WE GIGGLE AND LAUGH.

I CAN'T WAIT

TO SHOW YOU

MY SECRET HIDEOUTS!

MOMMY, PLEASE

DON'T CRY...

WHEN I FALL IT

DOESN'T HURT!

THERE ARE NO TEARS

IN HEAVEN.

"He will wipe every tear from their eyes.
There will be no more death or mourning or crying or pain,
for the old order of things has passed away."

I'VE MET A MAN NAMED NOAH.

HE TOLD ME ABOUT HIS BIG BOAT,

ALL THE ANIMALS, AND THE VERY FIRST

RAINBOW. HAVE YOU HEARD

OF NOAH, MOMMY?

MOMMY, PLEASE

DON'T CRY...

WE HAVE LOTS OF

PARTIES HERE;

WITH STREAMERS AND HATS,

AND THE BEST CHOCOLATE

CAKE EVER!

"Take heed that you do not despise one of these little ones, for I say to you that in heaven their angels always see the face of my Father who is in heaven".

WHEN IT'S TIME TO REST

ANGELS TUCK US IN,

I NEVER GET

SCARED MOMMY,

THERE IS NO

DARKNESS HERE!

JESUS IS

THE LIGHT OF HEAVEN.

MOMMY,

PLEASE DON'T CRY...

THE ANGELS ARE ALWAYS SINGING.

I LOVE TO SING WITH THE ANGELS!

YOU'D BE PROUD OF ME,

I HAVE A PRETTY GOOD VOICE.

I MUST HAVE GOTTEN IT

FROM YOU.

THERE IS A RIVER, MOMMY,

IN THE MOST BEAUTIFUL GARDEN

YOU COULD EVER IMAGINE...

AND A HUGE TREE WITH YUMMY FRUIT.

THE ANGELS CALL IT THE TREE OF LIFE.

MOMMY, IT'S SO WONDERFUL

TO BE ALIVE IN HEAVEN!

MOMMY, PLEASE

DON'T CRY...

SOMETIMES I JUST LIKE

TO BE BY MYSELF.

THAT'S WHEN I THINK OF YOU.

SOMEDAY, MOMMY, WE WILL

HOLD EACH OTHER TIGHT!

THEN YOU WILL CRADLE ME

IN YOUR ARMS,

AND STROKE MY HAIR...

AND ONCE AGAIN, OUR

HEARTS WILL

BEAT TOGETHER.

MOMMY, PLEASE

DON'T CRY...

I'LL WAIT RIGHT

HERE FOR YOU.

The Hope of Heaven

Heaven. Is there any place so inviting and at the same time so incomprehensible? What do you imagine when you think of heaven? The Bible tells us, "No mere man has ever seen, heard, or even imagined what wonderful things God has ready for those who love the Lord" (I Corinthians 2:9, TLB). Yet, it also tells us that heaven is a place of light, hope, and rewards. Jesus said, "I go to prepare a place for you." How marvelous to know a heavenly home awaits those who trust in Him.

My deep sorrow has given me a better understanding of the Bible and God's promises concerning heaven. Through the experience of losing my child, I have become more intensely aware of my heavenly home, and I live now in joyful expectation of going there someday.

I have often sat on my front porch and watched the beautiful sunsets, trying to envision what my little girl might be experiencing in heaven at that very moment: running and laughing, playing with other children, even walking with her great-grandparents. My precious child, and yours, is loved and cared for in that wonderful place called heaven. They are safe and secure in the arms of Jesus.

Knowing that my daughter is in heaven is one of my heart's greatest treasures. When I think about being with her again, my eyes often fill with tears of joy. I live with an overwhelming sense of hope and comfort as I anticipate that day.

You, too, can experience this same hope, comfort, and joy through a personal relationship with Jesus Christ. For the Bible clearly states that all who trust in His love, mercy, and forgiveness by faith are assured of eternal life in heaven. Therefore, you can know with absolute certainty that one day you will be reunited with your child.

A much-loved verse says, "For God so loved the world that he gave his one and only Son, that whoever believes in him shall not perish but have eternal life" (John 3:16). Jesus Himself said, "I tell you the truth, whoever hears my word and believes him who sent me has eternal life and will not be condemned; he has crossed over from death to life" (John 5:24). Those who trust in Jesus will be with Him forever in heaven one day!

Many years ago I invited Jesus into my life with a simple prayer like this…

Dear Jesus, I believe that You are the Son of God, and that You gave Your life for me on the cross as payment for my sins. I believe that You rose from the dead and that You are alive today in heaven. Please forgive my sins and come into my life as Savior and Lord.

Thank You for the gift of eternal life. Help me to trust You and walk with You here on earth until the day when I walk with You in heaven. Amen.

If you have sincerely asked Jesus into your life, He will never leave you. Nothing can separate you from His love. And because of this someday in that glorious place called heaven we will cradle and hold our children tight, and once again our hearts will beat as one.

I look forward to meeting you there!

Writing down my thoughts during quiet times of reflection helped me
along the path to healing, as I worked through my depression and pain.
These pages are provided for you to record your feelings and special remembrances.

MY THOUGHTS AND PRAYERS FOR YOU:

_____

_____

_____

_____

_____

_____

_____

_____

THESE WERE MY DREAMS FOR YOU:

_____

_____

_____

_____

_____

_____

_____

_____

_____

_____

BECAUSE OF YOU I HAVE LEARNED SO MUCH:

_____

_____

_____

_____

_____

_____

_____

_____

_____

_____

_____

In Memory of

_____

You Went to Heaven On

_____